EVERYDAY ORIGAMI

A Foldable Fashion Guide

by SOK SONG

CAPSTONE PRESS

a capstone imprint

GUIDE TO FOLDING

Making crisp, accurate creases is the key to a clean and polished origami model. Use these lines and symbols to help you and guide your creases. Don't worry if you've made a mistake or something seems confusing—just back up a couple of steps and try again.

LINES AND DASHES

- - - - - - - - - - - - - - - VALLEY FOLD

— · — · — · — · — · — MOUNTAIN FOLD

————————— CREASE LINE

· · · · · · · · · · · · · · · HIDDEN LINE

ACTION SYMBOLS

FOLD

FOLD AND UNFOLD

UNFOLD

FOLD BEHIND
(MOUNTAIN FOLD)

PLEAT

REPEAT

TURN OVER

SQUASH

MAGNIFIED VIEW

ROTATE

DISTANCE

FOCAL POINTS

DIFFICULTY LEVEL

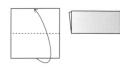 EASY

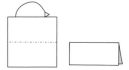 MEDIUM

  CHALLENGING

COMMON FOLDS

VALLEY FOLD
Fold the paper to the front so the crease is pointing away from you, like a valley.

MOUNTAIN FOLD
Fold the paper to the back so the crease is pointing up at you, like a mountain.

SQUASH FOLD
Open the pocket and squash down flat. Most often, this will be done on the existing pre-creases.

INSIDE REVERSE FOLD
Fold the flap or corner to the inside, reversing one of the creases.

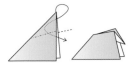

OUTSIDE REVERSE FOLD
Fold the flap or corner to the outside, reversing one of the creases.

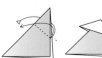

PLEAT FOLD
Fold the paper to create a pleat.

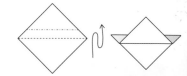

TABLE OF CONTENTS

Miniskirt 4

Maxi Skirt 8

Pleated Skirt 12

Jeans 18

Shorts 22

Skinny Pants 26

Sweater 30

T-shirt 34

Crop Top 40

Blouse 44

MINISKIRT

Anyone can pull off a **miniskirt** with the right attitude! An A-line miniskirt (like this paper version, which flares away from the body) tends to be the most flattering on all body types. Since miniskirts show off a lot of leg, it's imporant to balance that with a top that offers more coverage. It's also important to wear the right shoes. Flats will give your miniskirt a sweeter, more feminine look, while boots will offer a tougher edge.

STYLE TIPS

- To balance the shorter skirt, opt for a full-coverage top, such as a long-sleeved blouse, T-shirt, or jacket.

- Pair your miniskirt with tights or leggings to make it through cooler weather.

How To Fold

1

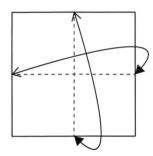

Fold the paper in half in both directions and then unfold. (Note: The side facing down will become the outside of the miniskirt.)

2

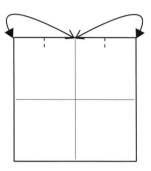

Bring the outside edges into the center crease and pinch a crease on only the top edge on both sides.

3

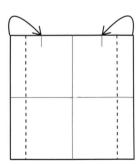

Fold the side edges into the pinch creases made in the previous step.

4

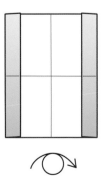

Turn the paper over.

5

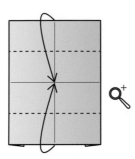

Fold the top and bottom sections into the center crease. (Note: The next step is a magnified view.)

6

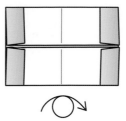

Turn the model over.

7

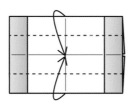

Fold the top and bottom edges, through all layers, into the center crease.

8

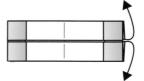

Gently pull out the bottom layers underneath and make the model flat. (See the next step for reference.)

9

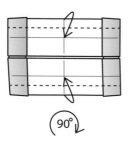

Fold the top and bottom edges to the upper and lower existing creases. Rotate the model 90°.

10

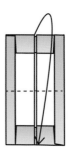

Fold the top edge down to meet the bottom so the paper is folded in half.

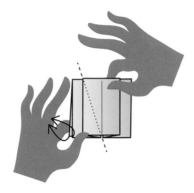

While pinching the top right corner section, pull out the bottom left corners in a swivel. Create the shape of the skirt by making the bottom wider.

Repeat on the opposite side.

Shape the waist of the skirt by folding the flaps sticking out on the top in on a diagonal. (Note: You can also fold a narrow waistband to hold them in place.) Turn the model over.

Enjoy your finished miniskirt!

MAXI SKIRT

Maxi skirts can work in spring, summer, or fall, depending on how you choose to style them. Pair your skirt with a tank top and flip-flops in the summer, or a sweater or jean jacket to make it work year-round, especially in cooler fall temps. One of the easiest ways to make a maxi skirt pop is with a bold print, like this paper version, which features bright colors and a fun pattern. You can fold the skirt so the stripes are horizontal or vertical, depending on your personal style preference.

STYLE TIPS

⊕ Opt for a maxi skirt that hits either just above or just below your ankles for the most flattering look.

⊕ Define your waist by tucking in your shirt or adding a belt to balance the flowiness of a maxi skirt.

How To Fold

1

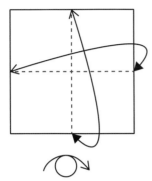

Fold the paper in half in both directions and unfold. Turn the paper over. (Note: The side facing down will become the outside of the skirt; the other side will become the waistband.)

2

Bring up the bottom edge to the halfway crease, and pinch only the corner section to mark it as a landmark crease. Unfold.

3

Fold the bottom edge to the landmark crease made in the previous step. Unfold.

4

Fold the bottom edge up to the new crease made in the previous step.

5

Fold the bottom edge up
again on the existing crease
to create the skirt's waistband.

6

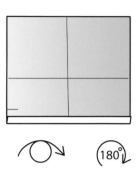

Turn the paper over and
rotate it 180° so that the folds
you just made are now at the
top on the back.

7

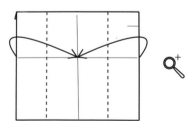

Fold the side edges into the
center crease. (Note: The next
step is a magnified view.)

8

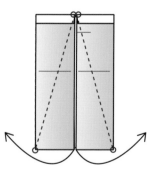

Fold the bottom corners
out on a diagonal.

9

Taper the waistline of the skirt by folding the top corners in at an angle.

10

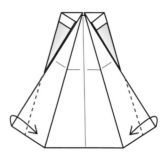

Shape the bottom of the skirt by folding the corners in as well.

11

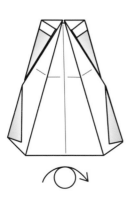

Turn the paper over.

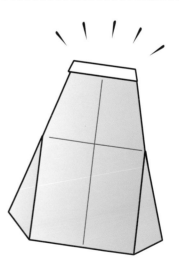

Enjoy your finished maxi skirt!

PLEATED SKIRT

Pleated skirts are a fun, feminine addition to any wardrobe. In order to balance the fullness of a pleated skirt, a fitted waistband is key. It's also important to choose a bright color or fun pattern to keep the skirt from looking too stuffy. This knee-length paper version utilizes an on-trend bird-print paper and complements it with a bright pop of color at the hem and waistband.

STYLE TIPS

- Pair your pleated skirt with a fitted T-shirt or blouse—make sure to tuck in whatever top you choose to show off the skirt's waistband!

- Wear with ballet flats for an easy, everyday outfit, or toss on a pair of heels to dress up your skirt!

How To Fold

1

Bring the bottom left corner up to the top left corner and pinch fold the center point, then unfold. (Note: The side facing up will become the outside of the skirt; the side facing down will become the contrasting hem and waistband.)

2

Fold the bottom corner up to the existing pinch crease to make a second pinch crease and then unfold.

3

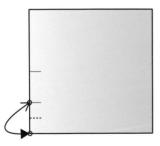

Make a third pinch crease by folding the bottom edge up to the crease made in step #2 and then unfold.

4

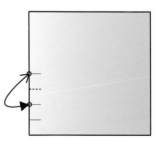

Pinch the midpoint between the center crease and the one below it and then unfold. (Note: You are dividing the bottom half of the paper into quarters.)

5

Fold the bottom edge up to the nearest pinch crease.

6

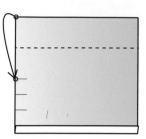

Fold the top edge down to the top pinch crease.

7

Turn the paper over.

8

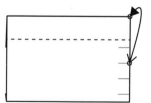

Fold the top edge down to the pinch crease just below the center crease and then unfold.

9

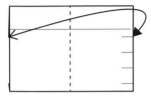

Fold the paper in half
vertically and then unfold.

10

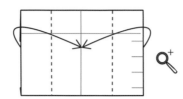

Fold the sides into the center
crease. (Note: The next step is
a magnified view.)

11

Turn the paper over.

12

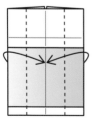

Fold the sides into
the center crease.

13

Turn the paper over.

14

Open the center flaps out
in the front. (See the next
step for reference.)

15

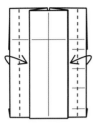

Fold the side edges into the folded edges.

16

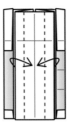

Bring the folded edges of the center section into the center crease.

17

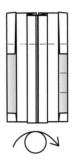

Turn the paper over.

18

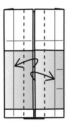

Bring the center folded edges out to the existing crease.

19

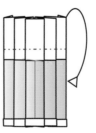

Mountain fold the top section to the back on the existing pre-crease. This should create an even color-changed band on both the top and bottom of the skirt.

20

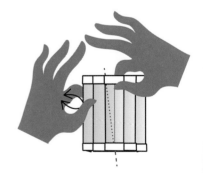

Pinch the top right sections together, and pull the bottom left corners together at the same time in a diagonal swivel. (Note: This will spread the bottom of the skirt into a wider base.)

21

Move out to the next layer of pleats and repeat the diagonal swivel. (Note: The objective is to spread the bottom of the skirt out while swiveling the top section up.)

22

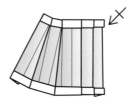

Repeat steps #20 and #21 on the opposite side.

23

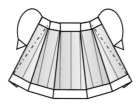

Mountain fold the sides to the back on a diagonal to shape the top of the skirt.

Enjoy your finished pleated skirt!

JEANS

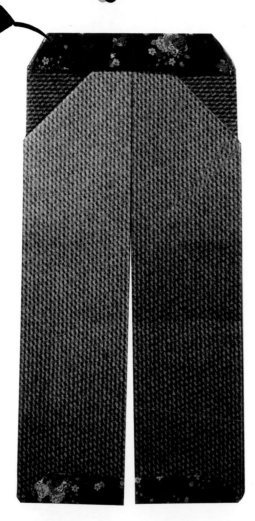

Believe it or not, **jeans** have been around since the 1800s! This essential garment has gone through a serious style evolution in the past fifty years alone—flares, bell-bottoms, straight leg, skinny leg, and high-waist, just to name a few. Jeans today can be incredibly unique—from colored, patterned denim to perfectly distressed pairs. But no matter your style, the perfect pair of jeans is a must-have.

STYLE TIPS

- Jeans go with anything! Pair with heels for a night out or dress yours down with flats for a casual, everyday look.

- Blouses, sweaters, T-shirts, and jackets all work well with jeans—choose whatever you want to create your own personal style.

1

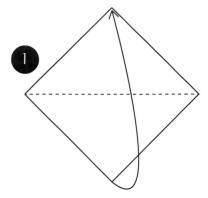

Fold the paper in half diagonally. (Note: Whichever side is facing down will become the outside of the jeans; the side facing up will be the waistband and cuffs.)

2

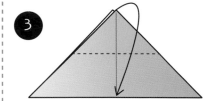

Fold the triangle in half and then unfold.

3

Fold the top corner down to the bottom. (Note: Only fold the top layer.)

4

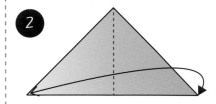

Fold both side corners up to the top point. (Note: The next step is a magnified view.)

5

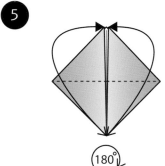

Fold the top corners (using only the top layer of paper) down to the bottom point and then unfold. Rotate the model 180°.

6

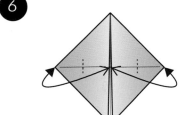

Pinch two landmark creases by bringing both side corners into the center and then unfold.

7

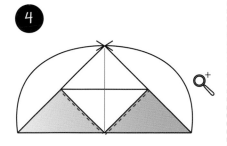

Fold the right corner to the landmark crease on the left side, make another pinch crease, and unfold. Repeat this step on the left side.

8

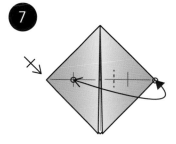

Fold the right corner to the nearest landmark crease on the left side and unfold. Repeat this step with the left corner.

9

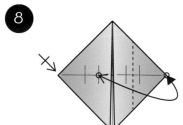

Fold and unfold diagonal creases on both sides by lining up the bottom side edges with the creases made in previous step.

10

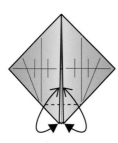

Fold the bottom triangles up and then unfold. Make these folds where the creases from steps #8 and #9 meet.

11

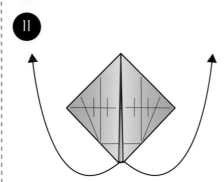

Unfold the top triangles back out to the sides. (See the next step for reference.)

12

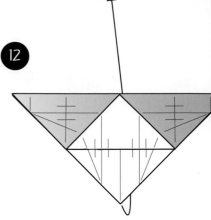

Unfold the bottom layer of paper to the back. (See the next step for reference.)

13

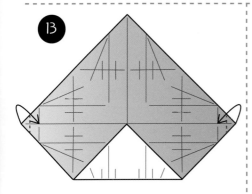

Fold the side corners in to meet the creases made in step #10.

14

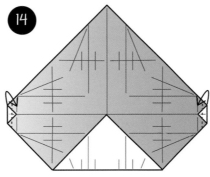

Fold in again, to the crease, through both layers.

15

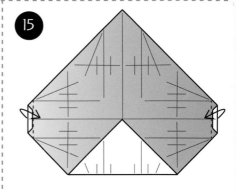

Fold in again, on the pre-crease. This will create a color-change cuff on the bottom of the jeans. (Note: If you don't want the color-change cuff, you can tuck the corners in on the other side.)

16

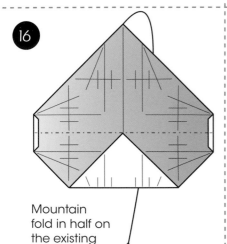

Mountain fold in half on the existing pre-crease.

17

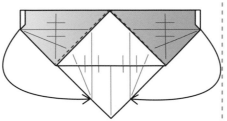

Fold the sides in along the pre-creases so the model once again looks like it did in step #10 with the cuffs folded in.

18

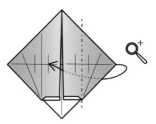

Inside reverse the right corner using the pre-crease from step #8. The tip of the triangle will stick out from the center. (Note: The next step is a magnified view.)

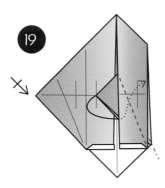

19

Using the diagonal pre-crease from step #9, inside reverse the triangle that is sticking out so it is hidden from view. Repeat steps #14 and #15 on the left corner.

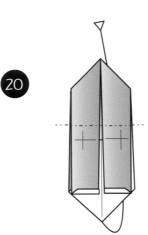

20

Fold the back section up as far as possible.

21

Fold the top corner down to the tip of the triangle point.

22

Fold the top edge down again.

23

Fold down again, overlapping the triangle points.

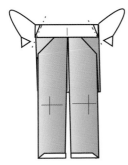

24

Mountain fold the corners to taper the waistband.

Enjoy your finished jeans!

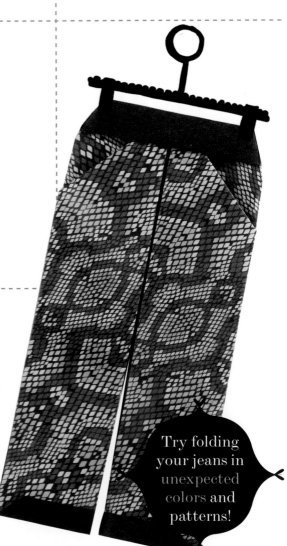

Try folding your jeans in unexpected colors and patterns!

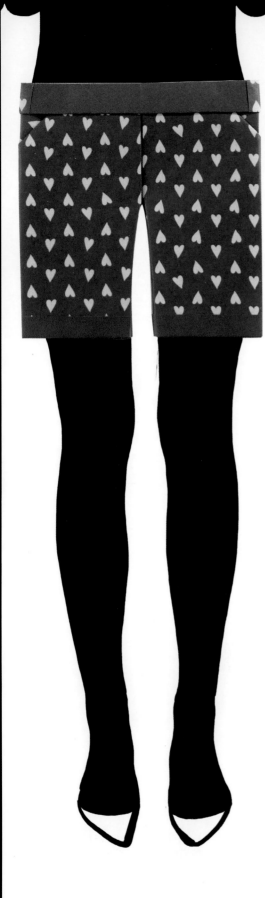

SHORTS

Just as jeans are a go-to garment in the cooler months, **shorts** are a summer staple. Shorts can be a great, versatile addition to any wardrobe because they come in a wide range of fabrics, colors, and patterns. From basic denim cutoffs to dressy linen pairs, shorts can act as the base for any outfit. This paper pair features a fun, whimsical pattern and contrasting cuffs, but you can fold them in a variety of patterns or solid colors depending on what you plan to pair them with. Experiment to create as many different outfits as you'd like! You can also adjust the length and width based on your own style choices.

STYLE TIPS

- Throw on flip-flops with your shorts for an easy summer look, perfect for bumming around!

- Pair your shorts with a T-shirt if you're going casual, or add a crop top or blouse for a slightly more fashion-forward look.

How To Fold

 1

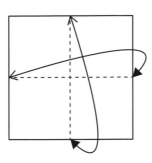

Fold the paper in half in both directions and then unfold. (Note: The side facing down will become the outside of the shorts.)

2

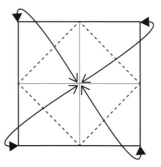

Fold all four corners into the center and then unfold.

3

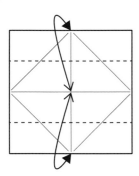

Fold the top and bottom edges into the center and then unfold.

4

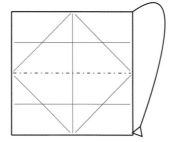

Mountain fold the paper in half to the back.

5

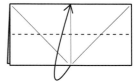

Fold the bottom edge up to meet the folded top crease.

6

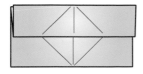

Turn the paper over.

7

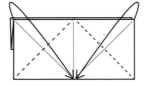

Fold the top corners down through all layers of paper.

8

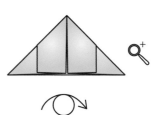

Turn the paper over. (Note: The next step is a magnified view.)

9

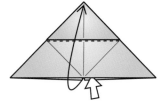

Lift the top layer and use the pre-creases to begin a squash fold.

 10

(Squash fold in progress.) Bring the center of the bottom edge up to the top point. (Note: The sides will also move up toward the top.)

11

(Squash fold in progress.) Use the pre-creases in the bottom layer to help lift the corners to the top point.

 12

(Squash fold in progress.) Flatten the corners to form a square. (Note: The next step is a magnified view.)

13

Turn the paper over.

14

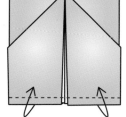

Fold the bottom edges up to make the cuffs. (Note: You can play around with the width of the cuffs by making this fold as wide or narrow as you'd like.)

15

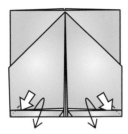

Open and squash each cuff so the contrasting color is visible. (See the next step for reference.)

16

Mountain fold the top triangle to the inside. (Note: Folding this down farther will create shorter shorts and a wider waistband.)

17

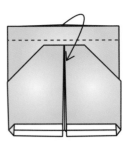

Fold the top section down to create the waistband.

18

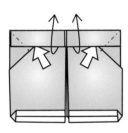

Open and squash the waistband so the contrasting color is exposed. (See the next step for reference.)

19

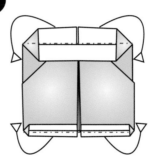

Mountain fold the top flaps on the waistband and bottom flaps on the cuffs to the back.

20

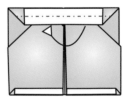

Mountain fold the top flap underneath to narrow the waistband.

21

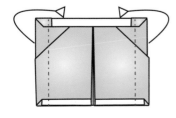

Mountain fold the sides to the back to narrow the width of the shorts.

22

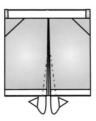

Shape and separate the legs by mountain folding the inside edges at a slight angle.

Enjoy your finished shorts!

SKINNY PANTS

Skinny pants are a great alternative to jeans when you want to spice up your look and try something different. This paper pair has a narrow leg and features a camo print, which can act as an unexpected neutral. Try folding the pants in a variety of colors and patterns to create an array of different looks. You can even use different textures to simulate leather leggings.

STYLE TIPS

⊞ Balance a narrow silhouette on the bottom of your outfit by pairing your skinny pants with a loose blouse or chunky sweater.

⊞ Ballet flats, high heels, and low ankle boots all work well with skinny pants.

1

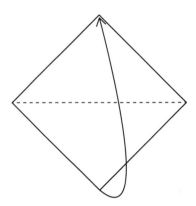

Fold the paper in half diagonally. (Note: The side facing down will become the outside pattern of the pants.)

2

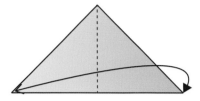

Fold in half again and unfold.

3

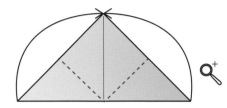

Fold both bottom corners up to the top of the triangle. (Note: The next step is a magnified view.)

4

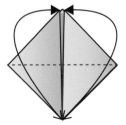

Fold the top corners down to the bottom and unfold.

5

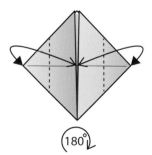

Fold both the left and right sides to the center and then unfold. Rotate the model 180°.

6

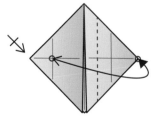

Fold the right corner to the crease on the left side and then unfold. Repeat this step on the opposite side.

7

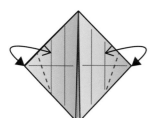

Fold a triangle on each side along the creases made in step #5 and unfold.

8

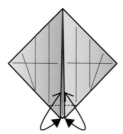

Fold the bottom corners up and then unfold. (Note: Use the creases made in step #6 as a reference for where to make this crease.)

9

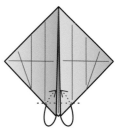

Inside reverse the bottom corners.

10

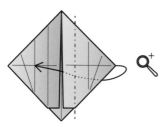

Inside reverse the right corner using the pre-creases from step #6. The corner will stick out on the inside. (Note: The next step is a magnified view.)

11

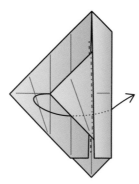

Inside reverse on the pre-creases made in step #5, so the triangle now sticks out to the outside.

12

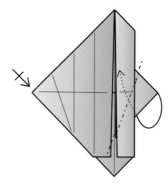

Using the pre-creases from step #7, inside reverse the triangle. Repeat steps #10–12 on the opposite side. (Note: There will still be a small point that will stick out on the sides.)

13

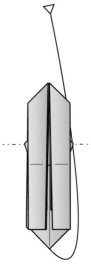

Mountain fold the back layer up as far as possible. (See the next step for reference.)

14

Fold the top corner down to create the waistband. (Note: The width of the waistband will be determined by how far you fold the paper past the center point.)

15

Fold the top edge down again to create the waistband.

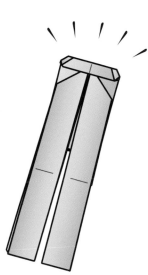

Enjoy your finished skinny pants!

16

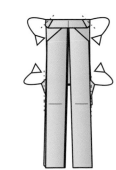

Mountain fold the top corners to shape the waistband, and then mountain fold the small triangular points that stick out on the sides.

SWEATER

A sweater can be a functional garment—keeping you warm and cozy in cooler weather—but it can also add a quick pop of color to any outfit. This simple paper cardigan uses both sides of the paper to create contrast. Try experimenting with the angle of the sleeves and the length of the collar/lapels to see what proportions you get in the finished product.

STYLE TIPS

- Toss a sweater over a T-shirt or blouse for a cool, layered look.

- Pair with jeans and flats for a casual outfit or a dress and heels for a fancier ensemble.

How To Fold

Fold a thin rectangle at the bottom of your paper to create a border for the lapels. (Note: The side facing up will become the outside of your sweater; the side facing down will be the contrasting lapels.)

Turn the paper over.

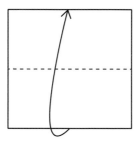

Fold the paper in half horizontally.

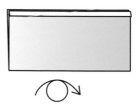

Turn the paper over.

5

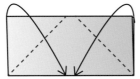

Fold the top corners down to the bottom, using both layers of paper. (Note: The corners will not meet in the center because of the border folded in step #1.)

6

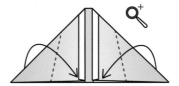

Fold the side corners in at an angle to create the sleeves. (Note: The next step is a magnified view.)

7

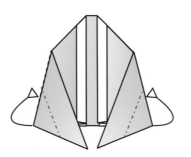

Mountain fold the side corners to the back to shape the sleeves. (See the next step for reference.)

8

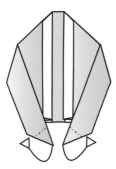

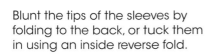

Blunt the tips of the sleeves by folding to the back, or tuck them in using an inside reverse fold.

9

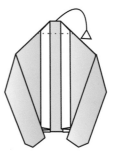

Optional: Fold the top section to the back to shape the collar, or leave it up depending on your preference.

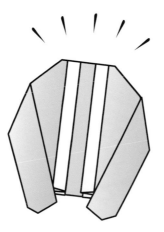

Enjoy your finished sweater!

T-SHIRT

T-shirts are one piece of clothing that never seems to go out of style. From basic cotton tees to luxurious silk styles, T-shirts can be worn in an endless number of ways. This paper version features an edgy pattern and a contrasting collar, but you can also try folding it in a floral paper for a sweeter style. Try several different patterns to make it your own!

STYLE TIPS

- Shorts or jeans pair perfectly with a T-shirt for a casual, relaxed outfit.

- Tuck your T-shirt into a high-waisted skirt for a fashionable, but still comfortable, look.

- Use your T-shirt as a layering piece; toss a sweater over the top to stay warm!

How To Fold

1

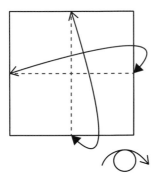

Fold the paper in half in both directions and then unfold. Turn the paper over. (Note: The side facing down will become the outside of your T-shirt.)

2

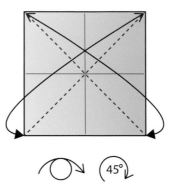

Fold the paper in half diagonally in both directions and then unfold. Turn the paper back over, and rotate it 45°.

3

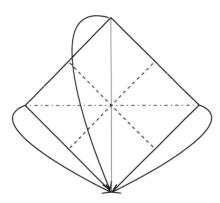

Collapse the model by bringing the top, left, and right corners together at the bottom using the existing pre-creases.

4

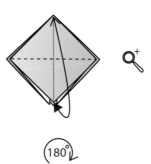

Fold the bottom corner up to the top and then unfold. Rotate the model 180° so the open section is at the top. (Note: The next step is a magnified view.)

5

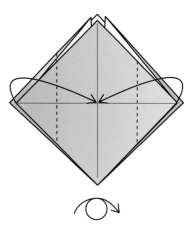

Using just the top two layers of paper, fold the side corners into the center crease. Turn the paper over.

6

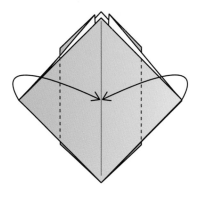

Fold the side corners into the center crease on this side, again using just the top two layers of paper.

7

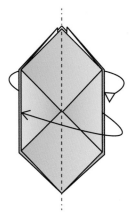

Rearrange the layers so the corners folded in the previous steps are hidden in between the layers. (See the next step for reference.)

8

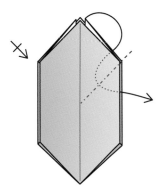

Pull the top, innermost corner out and down as far as you can. Use the folded triangles on the inside as a guide. Repeat on the opposite side.

9

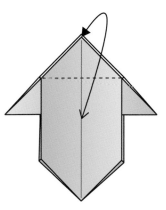

Fold the top triangles down (in both the front and back) and then unfold.

10

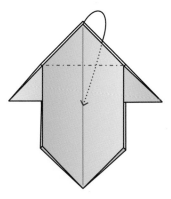

Mountain fold and tuck in the front layer so it is hidden inside.

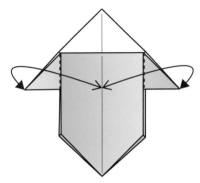

11

Fold the side corners in and then unfold.

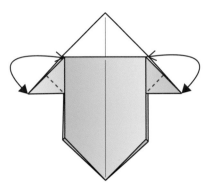

12

Fold the corners up, creasing the triangles in half, and then unfold.

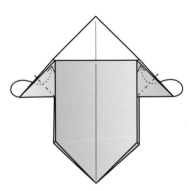

13

Open and then inside reverse the sides using the pre-creases, tucking the inner corners of the square inside. (Note: Just hide half of the square so a small triangle still sticks out.)

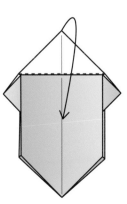

14

Fold the top triangle down over the front on the existing crease.

15

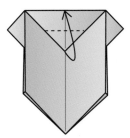

Fold the tip of the triangle back up to the top.

16

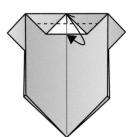

Fold the top layer in half through both layers of paper. Unfold the triangle back down to the bottom.

17

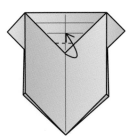

Fold the tip up on the first crease.

18

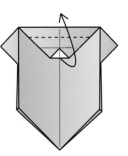

Fold the paper up on the crease closest to the top so that the top section sticks out and up. (See the next step for reference.)

19

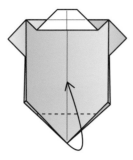

Fold up the bottom corner, making sure to leave a little bit of an angle on the sides.

20

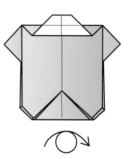

Turn the paper over.

21

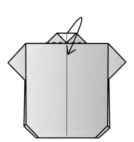

Fold the top trapezoid section down to form the collar/neckline.

Enjoy your finished T-shirt!

CROP TOP

Crop tops are a trend that keeps coming back. A crop top is a great, versatile garment because it can be either dressy or casual. This paper version has fun color-change sections for the midriff and lapels. Try folding in a variety of papers and patterns to reflect a dressier or more casual style.

STYLE TIPS

- Pair your crop top with shorts, a skirt, or high-waisted pants.

- Layer it over another top or blouse.

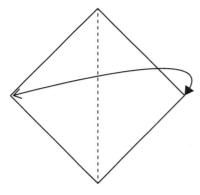

1 Fold the paper in half diagonally and then unfold. (Note: The side facing down will become the bulk of the crop top; the side facing up will be the contrasting sections.)

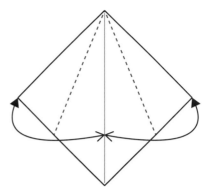

2 Fold the side edges into the center crease and then unfold.

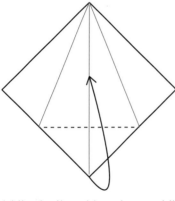

3 Fold the bottom triangle up at the bottom of the side creases.

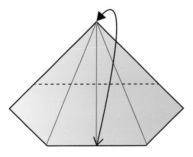

4 Turn the paper over.

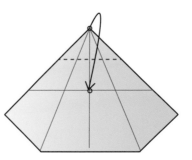

5 Fold the top corner down to the bottom edge and then unfold.

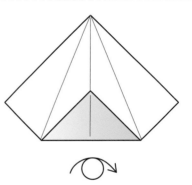

6 Fold the top corner down to the crease made in the previous step.

7

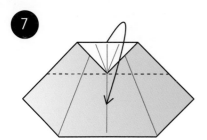

Fold the top section down on the existing pre-crease.

8

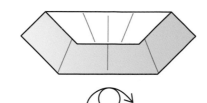

Turn the paper over.

9

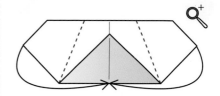

Fold both sides into the center on the existing pre-creases. (Note: The next step is a magnified view.)

10

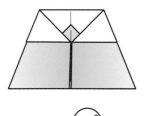

Rotate the paper 180°.

11

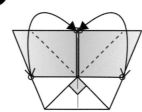

Using just the top layer of paper, fold the center corners down and out and then unfold. (Use the circled points for reference.)

12

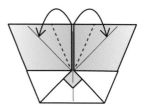

Fold the center corners out to the creases made in the previous step.

13

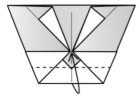

Fold the bottom edge up to where the paper changes color.

14

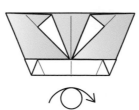

Turn the paper over.

15

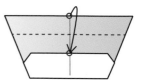

Fold the top edge down (through all layers of paper) to where the paper changes color.

16

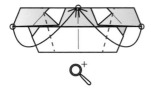

Fold the side corners in so they meet in the center at the top edge. (Note: The next step is a magnified view.)

17

Fold the triangle points back along the folded edge and then unfold.

18

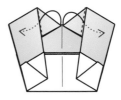

Tuck the triangle points inside the upper layer of paper. (Note: This is not an inside reverse—just tuck them under.)

19

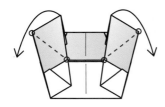

Fold the corners out along the indicated points to create the sleeves.

20

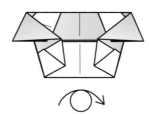

Turn the paper over.

21

Optional: Shape the bodice using a V-shaped mountain fold.

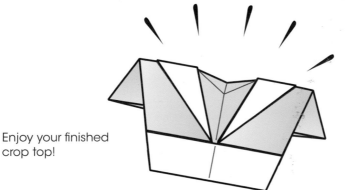

Enjoy your finished crop top!

BLOUSE

Blouses can come in many shapes and silhouettes, from sleek and fitted to loose and flowing. This paper version is accentuated by a contrasting collar and lapels, as well as modern, trendy cap sleeves and a peplum waist. You can play around with the size of the sleeves and collar by increasing or decreasing the size of the folds in steps #17 and #20. You can also eliminate the peplum by mountain folding the sides to the back on the finished model.

HOW TO USE

- Use your blouse to decorate the front of a fashion-forward greeting card.

- Let your paper blouse act as a stylish gift tag on a box or bag.

How To Fold

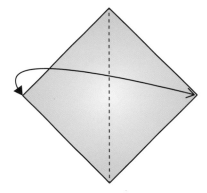

1 Fold the paper in half diagonally and then unfold. (Note: The side facing up will become the bulk of the blouse; the side facing down will become the collar and lapels.)

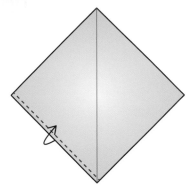

2 Fold a narrow rectangular flap on the bottom left side.

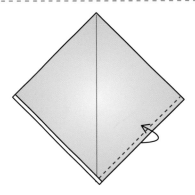

3 Fold an equally narrow rectangle on the bottom right side.

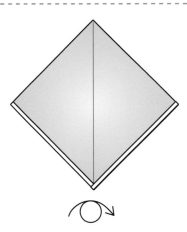

4 Turn the paper over.

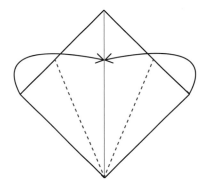

5 Fold the sides into the center crease. (Note: There will be a small, loose flap on the tip at the back. This will be folded inside later.)

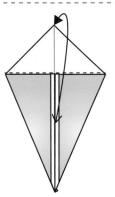

6 Fold the top triangle down and then unfold.

7

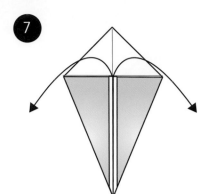

Unfold the side flaps.

8

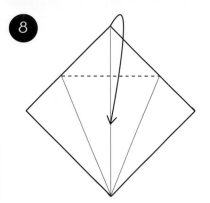

Fold the top triangle down on the existing pre-crease.

9

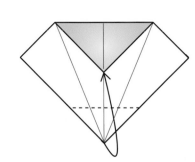

Fold the bottom point up to meet the tip of the top triangle.

10

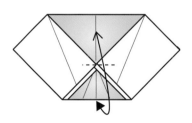

Pinch fold a narrow landmark crease where the two tips meet and then unfold.

11

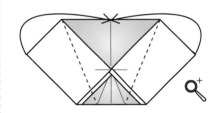

Fold the sides into the center on existing pre-creases. (Note: The next step is a magnified view.)

12

Turn the paper over.

13

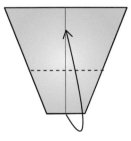

Fold the bottom edge up using the landmark crease made in step #10 as a reference.

14

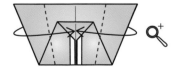

Fold the side edges into the center. (Note: The next step is a magnified view.)

15

Fold the top flaps out on a diagonal. (Note: Fold from the outside bottom corner to the upper inside corner.)

16

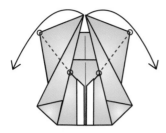

Fold the top corner flaps down to form the sleeves. Use both the corners and the circled point for reference.

17

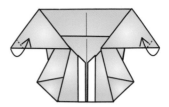

Fold in and blunt the tips on each side to shape the sleeves.

18

Fold in and blunt the top corners to shape the shoulders.

19

Turn the paper over.

20

Valley fold the top center corners down to make the contrasting collar.

Enjoy your finished blouse!

About The Author

Sok Song's passion for folding paper bloomed from a hobby he taught himself during childhood into an award-winning origami-design business called Creased, Inc. He later attended Parsons with the intention of incorporating his origami skills into garment construction and fashion design. Sok's work has been featured on numerous TV shows, including *America's Next Top Model* and *Extreme Home Makeover*. His work has also been included in magazines such as *Cosmopolitan*, *Elle*, *GQ*, *Harper's Bazaar*, *Icon*, *InStyle*, *Marie Claire*, *Pop*, *Self*, *Vanity Fair*, and *Vogue*. Other notable clients include Condé Nast Publications Ltd., Harrods, Macy's, Saks Fifth Avenue, The Museum of Art and Design, The American Museum of Natural History, and *The New Yorker*. Sok currently lives in New York City, although his folding work takes him all over the world.

Read More

Arcturus Publishing. *Fashion Origami*. London, England: Arcturus Publishing Limited, 2014.

Song, Sok. *Origami Outfits: A Foldable Fashion Guide*. Fashion Origami. North Mankato, Minn.: Capstone Press, 2016.

Savvy is published by Capstone Press
A Capstone Imprint
1710 Roe Crest Drive
North Mankato, Minnesota 56003
www.mycapstone.com

Designs, illustrations, and text © Sok Song 2016
Photographs © Capstone 2016

Library of Congress Cataloging-in-Publication Data is available on the Library of Congress website.

ISBN: 978-1-5157-1630-3 (library binding) — 978-1-5157-1647-1 (ebook PDF)

Summary: Ten original fashion origami garments, including everyday items such as jeans, shorts, and tops, complete with written instructions and illustrated diagrams.

Editor: Alison Deering
Designer: Aruna Rangarajan

Image Credits: Photographs by Capstone Studio: Karon Dubke, Sarah Schuette, studio stylist; Marcy Morin, studio scheduler; Author photo by Alexandra Grablewski
Folding Papers Textures: Shutterstock: AlexTanya, Anastasiia Kucherenko, Kumer Oksana, Olga Borisenko, OKing, Picksell, SalomeNJ, Studio Lulu, Svetolk, tukkki, Yudina,
Design Elements: Shutterstock: AlexTanya, Baksiabat, BeatWalk, Ivan Negin, Iveta Angelova, SalomeNJ, shorena, Svetlana Prikhnenko

Printed and bound in the USA.   009684F16